ADVENTURERS

OFF-ROAD BIKING

Jeremy Evans

CRESTWOOD HOUSE

New York

First Crestwood House edition 1992
© Julian Holland Publishing Ltd 1991

First published by Heinemann Children's Reference 1991,
a division of Heinemann Educational Books Ltd, Halley Court,
Jordan Hill, Oxford OX2 8EJ

Crestwood House
Macmillan Publishing Company
866 Third Avenue
New York, NY 10022

First edition

CRESTWOOD HOUSE

Design by Julian Holland Publishing Ltd

Printed in Hong Kong

1 2 3 4 5 6 7 8 9 10

Acknowledgments
Illustrations: Rupert White Studio, Martin Smillie.
Photographs: *a = above, m = middle, b = below*
All photographs were taken by the author except;
Cover, Mike Newton-MX (*front*), Evans Webb Associates (*back*); 6*b*, Andy Hooper-MX; 7*b*, Andy Hooper-MX; 8*a* David Eberlin; 17*m*, James Bareham-MX; 18*a*, James Bareham-MX; 19*m*, James Bareham-MX; 21*a*, James Bareham-MX; 26*a*, Andy Hooper-MX; 28*a*, 29*b*, Andy Hooper-MX; 33*a*, Local Motion; 35*a*, Local Motion; 36*a*, Evans Webb Associates; 38*m*, Andy Hooper-MX; 42*a*, 43*b*, Dan Cook; 44*a*, James Bareham-MX.

Thanks to Lester Noble of Orange Mountain Bikes and Stuart Sawyer of Local Motion for their help in supplying information and photographs.

Library of Congress Cataloging-in-Publication Data
Evans, Jeremy
    Off-road biking/by Jeremy Evans. — 1st ed.
       p.   cm. — (Adventurers)
    Includes index.
    Summary: Provides information about off-road biking, including the origin of the sport, equipment needed, safety and maintenance information, and riding instructions.
    ISBN 0-89686-687-4
    1. All-terrain cycling — Juvenile literature. [1. All-terrain cycling.] I. Title. II. Series: Evans, Jeremy. Adventurers.
GV1056.E93   1992
796.6 — dc20   91-13629
                                 CIP
                                 AC

Note to the reader
In this book there are some words in the text that are printed in **bold** type. This shows that the words are listed in the glossary on page 46. The glossary gives a brief explanation of words that may be new to you.

Contents

What is an off-road bike? 4
Born in the U.S. of A. 6
Going off-road 8
Choosing an off-road bike 10
The bike frame 12
What to wear 14
Riding safely on the road 16
Sense and safety 18
On the right trail 20
Off-road techniques 22
Keeping control 26
Riding in company 28
Route finding 30
Preparation and planning 32
Puncture problems 34
Clean up after every ride! 36
Regular care and repairs 38
Off-road racer! 40
The big events 42
The off-road classics 44
International associations 45
Glossary 46
Index 48

What is an off-road bike?

What is an off-road bike? Is it the same as a mountain bike or all-terrain bike (ATB)? They are all the same, recognizable by their big, fat, knobby tires, straight handlebars, powerful brakes and up to 21 gears. You need the gears to help get up very steep hills.

Compared to a drop handlebar road-racing bike, an off-road bike is much more rugged and tough. It can withstand the thumps and bumps of riding over rocky terrain. It also weighs slightly more. Although the name mountain bike is usually used to describe this kind of bike, a mountain bike is seldom used to ride up a mountain. Mostly, it is used on paved surfaces. Off-road or all-terrain bike better describes this new style of bike that first appeared in California 20 years ago.

Bike questions

Q: Do I need 21 gears?
A: Not all gears are usable since the chain is only really efficient when it's working in a straight line. Seven small **cogs** on the back wheel and three big cogs on the **chainwheel** provide a good selection of gears that will tackle most uphill and downhill slopes. Eighteen gears will perform almost as well as 21. It is possible that bikes will have even more than 21 gears in the near future.

The typical off-road bike

Off-road bikes may look similar to each other at first glance but can vary in many ways. Apart from the obvious choice of colors, there is a wide variation in frame materials, design and, of course, price. Top competition **custom bikes** are the most costly, with prices up to ten times as much as the popular models you find in stores.

The saddle is wide for comfortable riding.

Handlebars are almost straight and have powerful brake handles. There are two **thumb-shift** levers for the gears.

Cantilever brakes will stop a mountain bike in seconds.

Big, knobby tires give the best traction, or grip, on the ground without sliding. They do, though, have a lot of **rolling resistance** on paved roads.

The **quick-release lever** is used for taking off wheels.

Toe straps give a better grip on the pedals.

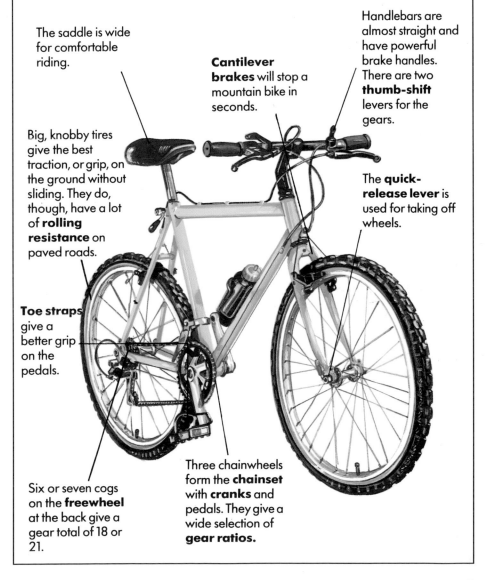

Six or seven cogs on the **freewheel** at the back give a gear total of 18 or 21.

Three chainwheels form the **chainset** with **cranks** and pedals. They give a wide selection of **gear ratios.**

Born in the U.S. of A.

Off-road bikes were first seen in Marin County (the San Francisco area of California) in the mid to late 1970s as a result of a downhill race on a track known as the Repack. This track dropped 1,300 feet in 1.8 miles, averaging a 14 percent gradient. Its surface featured all the classic off-road ingredients such as dirt, gravel, football-sized boulders and rutted stretches of bare rock. And 20 percent of it had very steep slopes. The race took close to four minutes. Conventional bikes couldn't handle this kind of treatment, so a new, heavily built style of bike began to evolve.

From then to now

The early Repack specials were adapted from old-fashioned bikes with balloon tires. Each weighed around 45 pounds – very heavy by today's standards. Gears were added so that the bikes could be cycled back up the hill. Since the hill was much steeper than any roads, the gearing had to be especially low.

From these beginnings the Repack racers began to build lighter bikes and to make other refinements. Americans began to take to off-road biking in large numbers. They had the wide, open spaces and miles of trails to use the bikes. They were also becoming more aware of sports and fitness. Big manufacturers soon became involved. By the time the new craze had spread across the Atlantic, the off-road bike was already becoming a highly technical, sophisticated, lightweight downhill racer.

Pushing the limits

Since the sport first started, off-road bikes have been where no one would have thought possible. Living up to the name of mountain bikes, they've been ridden and pushed to the top of all kinds of peaks, including Britain's highest mountain, Ben Nevis, Mount Olympus in Greece, and Kilimanjaro in Africa. They've been used to ride the rough roads from Alaska to Chile, across the width of Australia, and through remote parts of China. A mountain bike shop has even been opened in the Himalayas. They have their limits though. A good rider on a good bike can ride over frozen snow. However, once the sun starts to melt the snow on the mountain summits, your bike will let you know that it's time to get off and start pushing as the rider below has found out.

Bike questions

Q: Where are off-road bikes made?
A: When off-road bikes started to become popular, manufacturers from the Far East invested heavily in the new style of cycle. Most of the world's off-road bikes are now assembled in Taiwan and Japan. Most of the parts are also made in Japan. There are exceptions, such as Trek and Cannondale, custom bikes that are built to order in the United States. The **components** come from Japan.

Going off-road

Going off-road has the big advantage that it gets you away from cars, which are the biggest source of death and injury on the roads. It also gets you away from their smell and noise. It allows you to enjoy the countryside the way it should be. However, it's not always easy going, as the photograph above shows. Off-road trails vary from dirt tracks to boulder-strewn paths. Sometimes you may have no option but to carry your bike and walk. All good off-road bikes are light enough for you to be able to do this. They weigh 25 to 30 pounds.

Safety first

If in doubt, get off and walk. Experts can ride along boulder-strewn paths, but it's easy to catch a wheel rim and fall. You might land painfully on hard rock. On steep descents tripping the bike over a boulder can send you flying over the handlebars.

8

Types of trails

Other trail users

The best off-road trails are hard and flat for easy, fast riding. The worst trails are rough and rutted. The very worst is probably across a plowed field. The hard trail shown in the photograph below gives good traction but slows the riders down on the short but very steep uphill slope. They're competing in the MyCycles Classic in the Malvern hills of England.

The photograph was taken after a long period of dry weather. Riding in dry weather is always preferable. In rain the hard dirt track turns to mud. Apart from the rider's getting wet, rock and grass tracks become slippery. This creates problems in keeping traction uphill. If you share trails with horses, as is often the case, their hooves will churn the track into a bog that completely clogs up your chain and wheels.

Off-road you may well share the trails with hikers and horseback riders. Remember that they were using the trails first. The off-road bike is a newcomer that must treat them with respect.

The chief problem is that an off-road bike is much faster than hikers or horses when going downhill. You can have a great time speeding downhill at 25mph, but whatever you do don't scatter hikers and horses on the way. When you see them, slow down and let them by. Dismount if necessary. If they do wave you on give them a smile and thank them. In many parts of the United States, off-road bikers have been banned from trails. A few riders have failed to appreciate the rights of hikers and horses. They are represented by powerful groups, so treat them with respect.

Choosing an off-road bike

There is a vast choice of off-road bikes available at a wide range of prices. Urban mountain bikes are the cheapest. They may look as if they can be used off-road, but they are really more suitable for town riding. Their medium tires will help you get over the potholes, and the upright riding position lets you see over the traffic. A more suitable bike for hard off-road use will cost quite a bit more money. It should have at least 18 **indexed gears**, a light frame, steep frame angles for a good racing position, powerful **U-brakes** and cantilever brakes, knobby tires for traction in mud, and **sealed bearings** in the **hubs** and **bottom bracket**. The sealed bearings will stop the all-important **lubricating** grease from escaping. Lubrication keeps the parts of the bike moving easily.

Getting the right size bike

Bike sizes are measured in inches. It is important to get the right size for a comfortable ride. Finding the right size all-terrain bike is easy. When you stand over the frame with your feet flat on the floor, there should be three to four inches between you and the top tube. For a road bike this distance should be one to two inches.

10

Safety first

Whatever your age, you need a helmet for off-road riding. Modern cycle helmets are very light and comfortable to wear. The National Off-Road Bicycle Association, which governs mountain bike racing in the United States, requires helmets in its sanctioned events.

The rider in the photograph has the right size frame and the right seat height. He can put maximum power through the pedals, with an almost fully stretched leg at the bottom of each stroke. Stand astride a bike with your feet flat on the ground. Then allow four inches clearance between your crotch and the **top tube** of the bike. The top tube is the one running from the handlebars to the seat. This clearance allows you to vary saddle height. In addition, if you slip off the saddle there's enough room between your crotch and the top tube to cut the risk of painful landings.

Top tube clearance

The bike frame

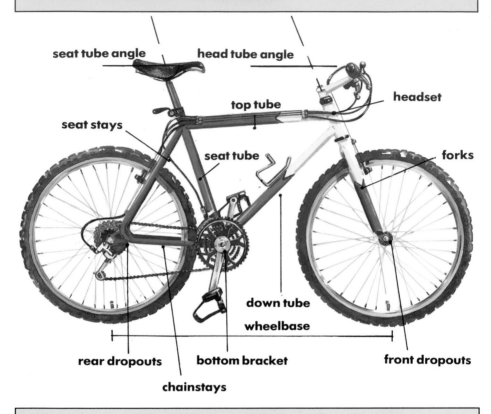

seat tube angle

head tube angle

headset

top tube

seat stays

forks

seat tube

down tube

wheelbase

rear dropouts

bottom bracket

front dropouts

chainstays

Frame shapes and materials

All frames are triangular, but the way the principal elements of the frame link up can vary. Small changes in shape can make a big difference in performance.

Compared to road bikes, off-road bikes generally need a higher bottom bracket for good ground clearance. The lower top tube should be well away from the rider. There should be straight handlebars for better control and riding comfort. Longer chainstays and wheelbase make the bike more stable. The most popular frame materials are **cro-moly** steel alloy tubing or plain steel tubing for the cheaper bikes. A few off-road bikes are made of aluminum tubing. This is lighter but not as strong, so the tubes need to be thicker than cro-moly ones. Steel frames are joined together by **lugs** or are **TIG welded**. All aluminum frames are TIG welded.

The illustration above shows how the elements of a frame link up to make a cycle, and how different angles between the tubes cause the shape.

Special features

The chain transfers power to the cogs on the back wheel of the bike. These cogs are made of steel and have cutout teeth to hold the chain. They fit onto a freewheel. This allows the back wheel to turn freely when you're not pedaling. Avid riders sometimes change the cogs to get different gear ratios. The number of teeth on each cog controls the number of gear ratios.

The pedals are attached to the cranks. The crankset holds the three chainwheels with which you drive the chain. These are often shaped as squashed circles rather than being completely round. They are supposed to make pedaling easier because they reduce the time that the cranks are vertical. The complete unit is attached to the bottom bracket of the frame by a steel **spindle** with sealed bearings.

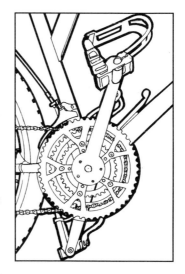

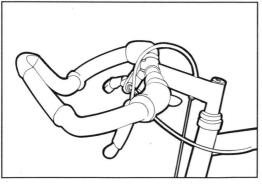

The **stem** connects the handlebars to the headset. Its length controls how far forward you have to lean to hold the grips. In road bikes, handlebars have special attachments so that you can get into a low position for fast riding.

What to wear

You don't have to wear fashionable fluorescent gear to ride an off-road bike, but it helps. You can wear conventional clothes, but they really don't work too well. Jeans are not flexible enough for easy leg movement. On the other hand, tracksuits are too baggy and are likely to catch on the saddle every time you stand up and sit down. Specially designed cycling shorts and tights are flexible and keep your body at the right temperature whether you're hot from riding uphill or cold from freewheeling downhill.

A shell helmet has a plastic outer shell and foam inside.

Eye protection is useful, but no good if there's mud flying about.

A lightweight cycling shirt with zippered neck has back pockets big enough to hold a map.

Gloves allow a good grip on the handlebars and protect your hands when you are riding close to bushes.

Lycra cycling shorts have a thick, padded crotch that makes sitting on a saddle really comfortable.

Cycling shoes with hard soles work well, as do lightweight hiking boots.

Additional clothing

Depending on the weather and how cold you get, you may need to wear additional or heavier duty clothing and accessories. Check out the list below:

● Boots or shoes should be water-resistant and worn with thick socks.
● When it's too cold for shorts, wear specially designed cycling tights with a thermal lining.
● Wear a thermal top jersey and a windproof jacket if necessary.
● Carry a lightweight cycling jacket on a waistband. It should be shaped to hang down behind the saddle to protect your backside from spray.
● The best gloves are made of a soft rubberlike material called neoprene. They are lined on the outside with Lycra, and the palms are made of leather. You cam remove the gloves once your hands have warmed up.

Safety first

● The more clothes you're wearing, the more protection you'll have if you fall. However, you can only wear so much in warm weather.
● The basic and most important safety accessory is the helmet. It must fit closely, with a chin strap that holds it on securely when you fall.

15

Riding safely on the road

Most off-road bikes have to be ridden on the road quite a lot. Here the main danger is from cars and trucks. Environmentalists talk hopefully of a time when cars and trucks will disappear and be replaced by quieter ways of getting around. Unfortunately, that's unlikely to happen soon. In the meantime cyclists have to live with vehicles.

Safe riding on the road needs thought, care and the correct tactics. In busy towns and cities the traffic may be dense, but the result is that it usually moves slowly. At 10mph you can keep pace with it. Show that you know you have a right to a place on the road and make your intentions clear. The off-road bike gives you a good upright riding position that lets you look over the roofs of small cars.

TIRES AND BRAKES
The thick tires have a large area in contact with the road so that they give exceptional grip. When you hit a pothole the wheels bounce out easily and let you ride on safely. Narrower tires specially designed for town use may be faster since they have less rolling resistance, but they are not as stylish and are of limited use once you go off-road. The true off-road bike has excellent brakes. With the gear thumb shifts on the handlebars your bike is well equipped for dealing with the challenges of riding in town and city.

After a great day out at an off-road event you've got to be prepared to ride on the road to get home. Remember to take it easy in traffic.

Be seen and be safe

Being seen is the main safety factor when riding on the road. Allow no motorists the excuse of saying "I never saw him." Wear the brightest cycling clothes you can find. A white or Day-Glo-colored helmet is better than a dark one. If you are riding at night or in conditions of poor visibility, you need good lights. You need a white one to show the way at the front and a red one that can be clearly seen at the back. The most versatile are clip-on battery lights that stay lit when you want them to. But some are not bright enough to be effective. Those fitted with rechargeable batteries are less expensive to run but can go out without warning when the batteries run down. Lights that run off generators are too heavy and tend to be difficult to fit to off-road bikes.

Using reflectors

Lights can be taken on and off, but you should also have permanently fitted **reflectors**. You need to have a red one mounted behind the saddle. The small reflectors on both sides of the pedals are very effective, as they can easily be seen bobbing up and down in the dark. Reflective strips attached to your clothing and helmet are a good safety feature when riding on the road at night or when it is twilight. Diagonal reflective belts that go across your back and chest are easily seen by motorists.

Sense and safety

BE SEEN
● During the day wear brightly colored clothing. At night wear white or reflective clothing and use a bright headlight and taillight. Wearing a helmet also makes you more visible and protects your head.

BE PREDICTABLE
● Ride on the right side of the road, with traffic. Stay far enough away from the curb to avoid parked cars, broken glass, potholes and other road hazards.
● Ride in a straight line, not weaving in and out around parked cars.
● Obey lane markings. Don't, for example, go straight in a right-turn-only lane.
● Yield to other traffic when going from a minor street to a major street or from a driveway into a street, and obey stop signs and red lights. Don't make any sudden moves if other traffic is around.
● Use hand signals to let other road users know what you want to do.

RIDE DEFENSIVELY
● Choose to ride on a route with few cars, slow traffic and easy-to-handle intersections. Choose streets that have room for cyclists and motorists to ride side by side.
● When moving from one lane to another, or even when changing positions within your lane, always look back first and yield to overtaking traffic.
● Look ahead for cars pulling out of driveways and for oncoming cars that might turn left in front of you.

Handlebar control

Your feet and legs provide the necessary **acceleration** when you need it. Your body helps you to corner as you lean into the turns. On an off-road bike, however, the handlebars are your control center. Your hands on the bars control the brakes and gears that govern how the bike will perform. A small pull on the levers should be all that is needed to put the brakes on completely. On off-road bikes the back brake is usually on the right handlebar, while the rear gear control is on the left. This allows you to brake and change down at the same time. You can adjust the **brake cables** using the small wheel on each brake handle as the **brake pads** wear down.

Bike theft

Off-road bikes are highly desirable. Because of this, they are often stolen. Make sure that your bike is properly insured against theft and serious damage. Check just what the insurance company will cover. They will almost certainly require you to lock the bike at all times. Cycle shops sell heavy-duty locks. In towns and cities you may also have to lock the wheels and remove your pump and other loose items when you leave the bike unattended. Sometimes saddles and seat posts get stolen as well. While you can't guard against all these things, you can leave your bike in well-lit places that will deter most thieves, and you can lock it to something solid that the thief can't remove. It's also worth checking how your local police can help safeguard your bike. In many cases they now have special markers put on to help identify stolen bikes.

On the right trail

An off-road bike can tackle most types of terrain such as grass, mud, rock, hard sand and sometimes even water, as you can see opposite. However, first you have to make sure that you are allowed to use the trail you have chosen. Most open country has plenty of tracks and trails, but these frequently go across private land. In many cases the public has the right-of-way to use them. This is shown on large-scale hiking maps and on signposts. These rights may only extend to hiking and not to off-road biking. Bikes are sometimes clearly shown to be banned from trails by signposts, which you must respect. Sometimes motorized trail bikes will be allowed to use the same trails.

The off-road code

● Ride only where you know you have a legal right.
● Always yield to horses and pedestrians.
● Avoid animals and crops. If this is not possible, stay as far from them as you can.
● Take all litter with you.
● Leave all gates as you found them, which normally means closing them after you.
● Keep noise down.
● Don't get annoyed with people on the trail. It never solves any problems.
● Always try to be self-sufficient. Take enough food, clothing and a puncture repair kit.
● Never create a fire hazard.
● Avoid bunching up with other riders and obstructing the trail.
● Always tell someone where you are going and give an estimated time of arrival.

What to expect off-road

When riding off-road you must look ahead to try to see what is coming. Good eyesight is a great help in reading the track when going downhill fast. If your eyesight is poor you should be wearing glasses. The disadvantage of glasses is that when you're following other bikes in wet weather, they soon get caked in mud and become unusable. Contact lenses are a better choice.

What you're looking for is anything that could send you out of control. Deep ruts made by four-wheel vehicles and tractors are particularly dangerous in cold weather when they become frozen. Potholes that will trip the front wheel must always be avoided. Look out also for such dangers as fallen branches, ice or gravel.

Off-road techniques

Braking

Good brakes on an off-road bike are so effective that you need to use them with care. If you just pull them on fully, both wheels may lock, and you may skid and fall. You use your right hand for the back brake, and your left hand for the front brake. Always use the back brake a little before and more than the front brake. This will help avoid a front wheel skid that sends you over the handlebars.

Cornering

If the riding surface is smooth, you can corner fast by taking your weight on the pedals and leaning into the turn. Lean the bike as far as it will go. If it leans too much, stab the ground with your inside foot to make yourself stable again. You can use the back brake to make a skid turn by locking the back wheel. This is exciting, but you should not do it if it is likely to damage the track. Let go of the brake when the bike has skidded around to face in the new direction, and the bike will straighten out.

22

Making slow turns

Turning the bike slowly between rocks or trees needs as much skill as high-speed cornering. To stop the bike from falling, you must keep your weight over the centerline between the wheels. Select a low gear and stand up on the pedals. Lean your body out of the turn while you steer the bike into it. If it starts to fall, a quick pull on the front brake should push it back upright.

Wheelies

The front wheel lift, or **wheelie,** is an important technique for getting you and your bike past small logs and rocks or over humps. You lift the front wheel high enough to clear the obstacle. Then you drop it on top or on the other side while pedaling hard.

Select a **low gear** and steer straight. Stand up and lean forward over the handlebars just before the obstacle.

Straighten up, pull on the handlebars, and pedal hard. The joint effect will lift the front wheel.

Keep the front wheel airborne (up in the air), pushing on the pedals with your weight back. Drop the front wheel on or over the obstacle.

23

How to go uphill

The best way to go up most hills is to stand up on the pedals to get the most power, but keep your weight back to avoid slipping.

"No pain, no gain" is a good way to describe riding up a steep hill. It is all about endurance. You just need to keep spinning the pedals, forget about your aching legs and heaving chest, and keep on up to the top. An off-road bike will get up the steepest of hills, but some skill is needed. The first thing to get right is the gears. On a steady climb you should **change down** gradually. You should never be pedaling in too low a gear or you will soon become tired. Try to keep up the same **cadence** – the number of times a minute your feet turn the cranks. When it gets too hard, stand up in the saddle to give a few hard pumps on the pedals. Then change down to the next gear.

If you are suddenly faced with a particularly steep slope, change down in plenty of time, selecting a suitably low gear. Once on the slope you will probably be driving the pedals too hard to be able to change down any further without stalling the bike. Standing on the pedals will drive the bike harder in a **higher gear**, but it is more tiring than sitting down and pedaling in a lower gear. If the back wheel begins to slip, get your weight back over the saddle.

How to go downhill

When you go downhill keep your arms straight, feet firm against the pedals, and body weight spread over the back wheel to balance the bike.

A fast descent depends on keeping the bike under control. On a steady slope you can go for speed, using the highest gear and braking very little. As the slope steepens, you will need to use the brakes more, pumping them to keep your speed under control. Don't let the bike run and then pull on the brakes hard when you realize you're going too fast. This will send great shudders through you and the bike. It is a most uncomfortable way to lose speed. If the slope gets seriously steep, you will need to get your weight behind the saddle to avoid going over the handlebars. Stand on the pedals and lever yourself so your seat is right over the back wheel, using your body to steer the bike.

Safety first

● Watch your speed, particularly on blind corners.
● Slow right down for hikers and horseback riders.
● If the slope seems too steep or difficult, get off and walk.

Keeping control

Falling off

The most likely time to fall off is while going downhill. If the bike goes out of control while you're leaning back, experts say you can simply put your feet down, hop off and leave the bike to run away.

You can also fall while climbing very steep hills. To prevent this, get enough weight over the back wheel to keep it gripping but stretch forward to keep the front wheel from lifting. If this fails, putting your feet down to steady the bike on a steep hill is not always easy. You may find yourself hopping backward or even rolling downhill with the bike on top of you. To avoid this, stand on the pedals and lean forward over the handlebars. At the same time turn the bike across the slope. Put your foot down on the slope above the bike where the ground is nearest. Lean the bike over into the slope so that you don't slither back downhill. Now you will be able to get off and push the bike up to the top of the hill.

Safety first

If you're going to crash, push the bike away from you or jump clear. Bikes are hard and unforgiving if you land on them or they land on you.

Control in the air

If you hit a bump at high speed the bike may become airborne. You may also lose control if you don't steer straight. The rider above is using a special jump ramp and is showing perfect midair control with his weight finely balanced down the centerline. The way to take off is to ride hard at whatever you're going to take off on. Then lift the front wheel as you get airborne. Pull up your legs to lift the back wheel. Let the back wheel touch down first, with your legs bent to absorb the impact. Never land on the front wheel. It would make it impossible to get the bike back on course and could result in a bad accident.

Left: Losing control can result in a rough tumble in the dirt.

Riding in company

Riding with friends

If possible always ride in company. A small group of three or four riders is best. If there are many more you will tend to clutter up the track for hikers and horseback riders. Choose one of your group as team leader. He or she can decide which way to go, when to stop and what to do if there is an emergency. Riding in company allows you to pace each other up and down the hills. You can take turns being in front. Also, when you're not too sure where you are, it's a big help if you can pool opinions.

Safety first

● Always let someone know where you are going, when you are going and when you expect to be back. Off-road bikes generally travel quite slowly, so for hilly country work out your arrival time using an average speed for the ride of 3½mph. If the ride is on flat, fast tracks, your average may be much higher. Always overestimate how long it will take.
● Share tools, first aid kit, spare clothing, food and water to spread the load.

28

Joining a club

There are many off-road bike clubs that organize rides in company and competitive events for local members. By joining one you'll meet people who enjoy biking. You'll learn where to go and when to go. You will also improve your riding skills by watching better riders. Some members of the club are bound to be skilled mechanics. They will probably be willing to pass on their skills and lend you their tools. If there's a club near where you live, joining it may be the best way safely to make progress in the sport. Many clubs are linked to national bodies such as Britain's Cycling Federation and America's National Off-Road Bicycle Association. You can find their addresses on page 45.

If you have any legal problems, one of these national bodies may also be able to help. For instance, if you are knocked down by a car driver on the road and want to take action, they can give you or your parents advice on what to do. They represent the best interests of all riders. It may also be worth joining an on-road bike club, since they have the same interests.

The start of the British Nationals, Forest of Dean. By joining a club you can eventually take part in similar competitions.

29

Route finding

A few well-used off-road cycling routes can be followed by signposts alone, but generally you will need a map to show where you are and where you're going. In most countries all tracks and trails for off-road biking will be clearly shown on hiking maps. They are usually shown by dotted lines drawn on the map in a particular color. It is also important to get the right scale map. Usually the 1:50,000 scale is ideal. Two centimeters on the map represents one kilometer of a trail. Alternatively, the 1:25,000 scale where four centimeters equals one kilometer gives more detail.

Map reading

You will need to learn how to read maps and to use a compass. It is very easy to lose your way when riding over an area of moorland or wilderness, particularly if the sun is covered by clouds. A small, handheld compass is necessary to find out directions.

You should be able to find **grid references** and understand the symbols for roads, trails, information points and other general features shown on maps. You should also be able to read the contour lines on a map so that you know which way is downhill and which way is up. Knowing how steep the hills are likely to be is also important for off-road bikers. If you learn how to do these things you will be able to find new trails to enjoy with confidence.

Lost? Try to work out exactly where you are using your map and your knowledge of your surroundings.

Safety first

● Don't ride off-road on trails without first planning your route.
● Plan alternative routes in case something goes wrong.
● Take a compass, so you know in which direction you're heading.
● Take a map and follow your route along it as you go.

This shows a ride in England, half off the road, and half on the road.
1. Start at grid reference 698161 by the church at 120 meters above sea level.
Ride south uphill on the marked track. **2.** Cross the bridge and ride across
Flatlands, following the track across a stream. **3.** At the village of Burnton
(698139) start a climb to 728 meters on Smawdon Hill. **4.** Ride down to Rough
Bridge at 272 meters. **5.** At the next stream you may need to carry your bike
over, before the steep climb to High Crag at 625 meters (693113). **6.** After
another downhill ride, follow the track along the side of Cow Reservoir. **7.**
Cross the bridge at the head of the reservoir. **8.** Join the road at 670113, at a
height of 100 meters. **9.** Ride on around the road and across Hope Bridge to
your starting point.

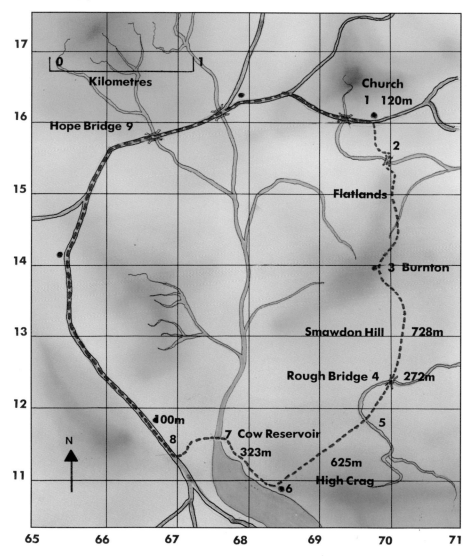

Preparation and planning

Panniers should be fixed to racks securely attached to the bike. The contents of the panniers should not be able to shift around while the bike is moving. The panniers should be waterproof, but if in doubt wrap the contents in plastic bags.

Pack the contents so you can get at what you need when you need it. Divide them into what you need for the trail and what is needed later when you stop or set up camp.

Low panniers are more stable than high panniers. However, they're likely to catch on the ground when you are riding through rough country.

Unless you're planning a serious trip lasting a few days, you won't need most of the gear required by the long distance off-road biker shown above. However, before leaving on even the shortest of trails, there is a bike checklist to go through. **1.** Brakes must be in first-class working order. **2.** Check **tire pressure** and tire wear. **3.** Check that the wheels fit tightly in the dropouts and that there are no broken spokes. **4.** Check that the saddle is the correct height and a tight fit. **5.** Check that there is no looseness in the headset. This tends to come loose in time. **6.** Check the pedals. **7.** Check gears and chain for rust and dirt, and lubricate as necessary.

Take the bag that suits you best to carry the necessary gear when you go off-road.

What to take on a long trip

PUNCTURES Take **tire levers**, spare **inner tube** for quick changes, pump, and puncture repair kit.

TOOLS Take a **chain tool** in case the chain breaks, plus 4/5/6mm **Allen keys** and the correct screwdriver for tightening things up. Some of these are in an all-in-one tool kit, available at most bike shops.

CLOTHING Depending on the likely weather, you should carry a windproof or waterproof top plus extra layers for warmth. Take gloves if you need them.

LIQUID It is vital to replace the liquid you lose through **dehydration** – loss of body fluid. Carry at least two water bottles that fit in the bottle cage on the bike. Refill as necessary.

FOOD You should prepare for a ride by eating well beforehand. The best fuel is high in calories and rich in protein. Pasta, cereal, bread and fruit are good. Take snacks for the ride. Bananas and raisins are good sources of energy, healthy and easily carried. Stop and snack frequently.

MAPS Plan your route beforehand so you know where you are going. Make sure you take the right maps for your journey. Take a compass too.

SAFETY One of your party should carry a small first aid kit. You should each take a whistle, in case you get lost in fog.

Puncture problems

Punctures are a part of off-road riding, but you don't get too many of them if you're careful. Check that your tires are in good condition. If you're riding over a rocky surface, make sure to **inflate** them (blow them up) fully. Hitting a small rock at speed with a soft tire will frequently blow the inner tube. Then you will get two punctures, one on each side of the wheel rim. Small pieces of broken glass may also get picked up in the tire and cause a puncture.

Mending punctures

As soon as you realize you have a puncture, stop and get off. Riding on a flat tire is not only dangerous, but it will damage both the tire and wheel rim.

1. Take the wheel off and **deflate** the tire completely.

2. Use the tire levers to lever one side of the tire off the rim, taking care not to tear the inner tube.

3. Remove the inner tube, check for thorns, and replace with the spare tube that you should always carry.

4. Push the rim of the tire back on, using the tire levers as necessary.

5. Put the wheel back on the bike and inflate the tire.

If you have to use a puncture kit, you should blow up the punctured tube as fully as possible. Listen for the hissing of escaping air to find the leak. Then apply a patch.

Muddy problems

A muddy ride can be fun, but there are things to look out for as you slip and slide around. If you get soaking wet from spray and from falls, you can get extremely cold in a short time. Remember that there's a big temperature difference between downhill and uphill riding. If your ride is downhill all the way home in the late afternoon, beware. It can get very cool when the sun goes down.

The best thing about mud is that it slows you down and helps cushion hard falls, so you don't get hurt. In fact, injuries while riding off-road are uncommon. It's always wise, though, to take a first aid kit to deal with minor cuts and scrapes. If one of your party is more badly hurt, send someone to get help.

Broken chains

Chains occasionally break unexpectedly. Without a chain tool you have no means of mending the chain and will have to push your cycle all the way home. The chain tool is a small tool for removing the broken link and rejoining the two ends of the chain. The fact that the chain is now shorter doesn't matter, as the **derailleur spring** will take up the extra tension. However, if the chain has broken once it may soon break again.

Safety first

● Check the weather forecast.
● Time your ride so you finish well before dark.
● Carry everything you need for mending punctures, as well as basic tools such as a chain tool.
● Carry a small first aid kit, and make sure you know how to use it.
● Always ride in company. It's more fun and is safer.

Clean up after every ride!

Off-road bikes have the hardest life of any cycles. The cyclist in this photograph is riding across the dry and dusty terrain of the Canary Islands. In dry weather the gears and chain soon become packed with dust and dirt. These grind their way through the mechanism. After a wet weather ride, the mud clings to your bike and will stay there and turn every moving part rusty unless quickly removed. You can't expect to ride your bike hard off-road and then just put it away and leave it until the next ride. It needs plenty of care. This should start as soon as you've finished riding.

How to clean your bike

Mud is the great enemy, and water removes it faster than any other means. The quickest way is to use a power hose. Take care not to use the highest blast setting. That is powerful enough to peel off chipped paint. There's also a danger it will wash out the grease from the sealed bearings, which are never totally watertight. A conventional hose or even a bucket of warm, soapy water will do just as well. Use a soft brush. Wash both sides of the bike and then turn it upside down to get at the underside. If necessary remove the wheels so you can clean the forks and chainstays properly. Then leave the bike to dry. Use a clean rag to wipe any remaining grime and grease from the frame.

Everyday care

You should aim to keep your bike looking and performing like new. When it has dried off after washing, you'll need to replace all the lubricating oil that has been washed off. The chain and **rear sprockets** should be oiled almost every time you ride. Other moving parts of the bike can be left for longer. The lubrication diagram on page 39 shows how to do this. A light lubricant put on with a spray-on can is best for everyday use. You simply wind the pedals backward while you spray the lubricant onto the chain as it passes over the **sprockets**.

Safety first

A badly maintained bike is a dangerous bike. Left dirty and unlubricated, the chain will jump off the sprockets, the **gear cables** will become blocked, and the **brake blocks** will jam on the rims. You will have an unsatisfactory ride even if it isn't dangerous. So always take time to care for your bike.

Regular care and repairs

If you ride your bike hard, you should inspect it once a week.

CHAIN Clean the chain with a rag soaked in spray lubricant. Adjust stiff links with a chain tool.

TIRES Check for general wear and **sidewall** damage.

WHEELS If a wheel is out of line or dented, it needs to be adjusted with a **spoke wrench**.

CRANKS Check that the cranks are tight.

GEARS Check that the **derailleur** is lined up properly.

Checking brakes

Good brakes are essential. Check that the blocks are correctly lined up with the rim. If the blocks are badly worn on one side, turn them over. If they are badly worn on both sides, replace them. Brake cables need regular lubrication to make sure they run freely. Check the cables for wear. If the **spring return** on the brakes isn't working well, it means the brakes are clogged with dirt. They will need to be stripped down and cleaned.

Lubrication

Cleaning, lubrication and minor adjustment are what bike care is all about: **1.** Clean the **derailleur jockey wheels** and gear cogs, and lubricate. **2.** Lubricate freewheel by laying the bike on its side. **3.** Clean and lubricate the chainwheel gear mechanism. **4.** Lubricate the cables for both sets of gears. **5.** Lubricate the brake cables. **6.** Lubricate **brake pivots**. **7.** Lubricate bottom bracket by pouring oil down the top tube. **8.** Lubricate pedals by taking off end caps.

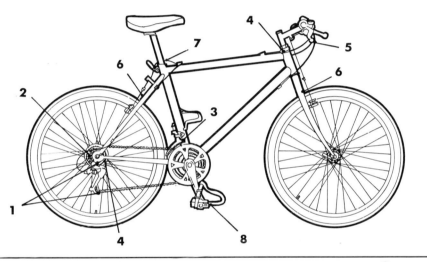

Tools for the job

The most important tools are the ones you take off-road, shown here on the right. For minor breakdowns you should always carry a puncture repair kit, tire levers, 4/5/6mm Allen keys, a small adjustable wrench, and a chain tool. You will also need a bigger adjustable wrench and screwdrivers for working on the bike at home. If you want to buy more specialist tools, you should get a **crank extractor** for undoing cranks, a spoke wrench for adjusting wheel spokes, and a **C-wrench**.

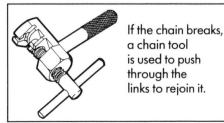

If the chain breaks, a chain tool is used to push through the links to rejoin it.

Off-road racer!

Off-road racing has now caught on in a big way throughout Europe and the United Kingdom. It's a tough, rough sport that takes a lot of determination and stamina. If you try it, you and your bike will face some challenging tests. Riders are divided into suitable classes. For some competitors winning is all, but most people just like to be part of the racing experience. Most big events have a carnival-style atmosphere, and entries of 400 or more bikes are common. To add to the fun there are often shops, stalls and sometimes even clowns riding unicycles to amuse the crowds.

Safety first

● When racing you must wear a suitable protective helmet.
● Only use fat tires. They will give you better control and are kinder to the environment.
● Make sure your bike is in tip-top condition.
● Keep out of trouble by avoiding crashes.
● Make sure you are properly insured.

Classes and competitions

If there's a large entry, riders are usually split into Professionals, Amateurs, Veterans, Novices, and Juniors with their own under 16 and under 18 classes. The rider below is one of the under 16 class at Britain's annual MyCycles Malvern Classic. He's tackling one of the short, steep hills of the four-mile up-and downhill course. The professionals go around six times to make it a real marathon. Most races have a much shorter course, usually up to two miles long. Riders take part in heats leading through to semi-finals and finals. Depending on the number of laps, each heat may only take 20 minutes. Riders go flat out all the way, avoiding the seemingly inevitable crashes and pacing themselves to the finish line.

The big events

Riders compete in a wilderness race in the World Championship at Durango, Colorado.

Wilderness and trials riding

As well as short course races, there are long wilderness or cross-country races. These are usually about 20 miles long and may take several hours of hard riding. The rides are split into classes and each class starts together. Warming up before the start is important so that you can get going quickly. You set your own pace in these tests of off-road biking endurance. Once out on the course you must use your skills, overtaking carefully, letting faster riders by, and keeping out of trouble. Sometimes, if the course is poorly marked, your knowledge of navigation may be needed as well.

A very different skill is trials riding, where riders show off their bike-handling skills. Entrants tackle the course one by one. It's only a short distance, but it is divided into different areas of difficulty. These usually include seemingly impossible obstacles such as big logs to jump, near vertical descents, and super-slippery hills. Trial riders need to be experts in the use of wheel traction, selection of the right gears, precise use of the brakes, and continuous movement of body weight. Putting a foot down loses you points. The top riders use specially made bikes. They have very high bottom brackets for maximum ground clearance and small wheels.

Downhills and uphills

For speed lovers, the greatest thrill is downhill racing, where one by one the riders race downhill against the clock. This is a test of skill and courage. It depends on your ability to judge the track surface correctly, and to get around the corners, which demands good eyesight. This type of race will test you and your bike to the limits. Injuries are common, so approach any downhill race with great care.

A refinement of the downhill race is the dual **slalom**, based on snow-skiing competitions. Two riders race downhill on a parallel course alongside each other, slaloming their bikes through "gates" marked by flags. The course is short, so you have to start very fast, then let the bike go, and rely totally on your cornering skills to make it to the bottom first.

At the other end of the scale come hillclimbs. These need stamina, endurance and technique. Riders leave the start line one by one and have to race to the top of a hill against the clock. There are usually two kinds of course. In the first the hill is ridable all the way and is likely to be a long-distance climb up a hillside. The race may take an hour or more to complete. This demands great stamina and determination. The second style of hillclimb demands great technique. It takes the form of a sprint up a short slope, parts of which may be almost impossible to ride. If no one makes it to the top the winner is the rider who gets farthest up the hill.

Less intense forms of off-road competition are orienteering, where navigation is the key skill, off-road treasure hunts where you follow a set of clues, and fox and hounds where one rider is pursued by the pack.

The Leaping Lizard Freefall Downhill is held annually in Laguna Hills, California.

The off-road classics

Riders all start together in a Grundig Series race, one of Europe's classics.

As the world's first off-road biking nation, the United States has several classic sites for hillclimb, downhill, dual slalom, and cross-country marathon racing. These include Mammoth Lakes and Big Bear, in California, and Durango, in Colorado, which hosted the 1990 Mountain Bike World Championship. Around 1,200 entrants took part. The National Championship is the top event of the National Off-Road Bicycle Association (NORBA) each year. In Europe the most important events are a series of around half a dozen big meetings sponsored annually by Grundig. These range from hillclimbs in the Alps to a regular event in Britain. Crystal Palace in London and Aviemore in the Scottish Highlands have both been used.

THE PROFESSIONALS
All the top riders on both sides of the Atlantic are professionals. Their equipment is provided by the bike and accessory manufacturers, though they almost always use custom-built frames. Some of their earnings comes from prize money, though they tend to earn much more from outside sponsorships.

The champion of all off-road racers is Ned Overend, the American rider for Team Specialized. He won the World Championship in 1986, 1987 and 1988. He failed in 1989 when he had the flu but won again in 1990, when for the first time the top American and European events were combined. Before that both continents had held their own world championships.

John Tomac, another American, is almost as famous. He rides for Team Mongoose. He is known for his larger-than-life personality as well as for being a consistent winner of the NORBA Series. When it comes to the World Championship, though, he has never managed to beat his archrival, Ned Overend. On the other side of the Atlantic, Tim Gould from Sheffield, England, is acclaimed as one of the finest riders in the world. He rides for Team Peugeot. Like many of the top Europeans he learned his skills through cyclo-cross. In cyclo-cross, running and riding are combined, using conventional racing bikes on off-road courses. Tim has dominated national competition. Internationally his biggest successes have included winning the Hillclimb World Championship at Mammoth Lakes in 1989. This involved a four-mile mountain climb, from 8,000 to 9,000 feet. Tim Gould's biggest competitor on the Grundig circuit has been Mike Kluge from West Berlin. A former Amateur Cyclo-Cross World Champion, he won the Grundig series in 1990.

The hall of off-road fame would not be complete without Mike Kloser of Alpine Stars. Mike was a consistent top finisher in the United States for a number of years before he decided to compete almost entirely in Europe. In 1988 he won the European version of the World Championship. He took the lead when Tim Gould had a puncture and Ned Overend burned himself out while racing at the head of the pack. Mike's specialty has been the Idata Bike Race, which he has won twice. Some call it the "Idiot Bike Race," because it is held across 200 miles of Alaskan snow.

International associations

Bicycle Federation of America
1818 R Street NW
Washington, DC 20009

Bicycle Federation of Australia
399 Pitt Street
Sydney NSW 2000, Australia

Bicycling Plus Mountain Bike
33 E. Minor Street
Emmaus, PA 18098

Bikecentennial
P.O. Box 8308
Missoula, MT 59807

British Cycling Federation
70 Brompton Road
London SW3 1EN, UK

Canadian Touring Cycling
  Department Association
333 River Road
Vanier, Ottawa
Ontario K1L 8B9, Canada

International Mountain Bicycling
  Association
Route 2, Box 303
Bishop, CA 93514

National Off-Road Bicycle
  Association
1750 E. Boulder
Colorado Springs, CO 80909

Glossary

accelerate, acceleration: go faster
Allen keys: important tools in different metric sizes, which are used to screw and unscrew bike fittings
bottom bracket: the hole in the base of the frame, where the chainset is attached
brake blocks: the rubber blocks that are squeezed against the rim
brake cables: the wire cables that connect the handles to the brakes
brake pad: see **brake blocks**
brake pivot: where the brake arms rotate
C-wrench: specialist tool for headset
cadence: the number of times the feet turn the cranks each minute
cantilever brake: a brake with two arms that are pulled upward
chainrings: the big cogs driven by the chain from the bottom bracket
chainset: the unit, comprising chainrings, cranks and pedals, which is fitted into the bottom bracket
chainstay: the two narrow frame tubes that extend backward from the bottom bracket. Some off-road bikes feature arch-shaped elevated chainstays that attract less mud
chain tool: tool used to mend broken chains
chainwheels: see **chainrings**
change down: changing from high gears to lower gears as a rider goes uphill or negotiates a tricky trail
cogs: circular toothed wheels driven by the chain
components: a collective name for all bike hardware including chainset, pedals, cogs, gears and brakes
crank extractor: a specialist tool used for removing cranks
cranks: the arms that drive the chainwheels

cro-moly: chrome molybdenum alloy steel tubing is used in the construction of most superior off-road bike frames. Reynolds 531 tubing is a well-known brand of manganese molybdenum favored by custom builders, as is lighter Reynolds 753
custom bikes: bikes that have hand-built frames, made to measure
deflate: let the air out of a tire
dehydration: drying out due to not drinking enough when overheating
derailleur: the arm that hangs below the cogs on the back wheel. It is moved in and out by the gear shifter, lifting or dropping the chain onto a different cog
derailleur jockey wheels: the two little wheels that guide the chain through the derailleur
derailleur spring: the spring that allows the derailleur to move inward to change gear
down tube: the diagonal tube connecting the bottom bracket to the headset
dropouts: the cutouts in the front forks and chainstays where the wheels fit into the frame
forks: the two front forks hold the front wheel. Fork offset, which is the amount the fork dropouts extend forward, is important to handling
freewheel: a block that fits into the wheel hub, allowing the chain to drive the wheel forward without the wheel driving the chain forward
front dropouts: see **dropouts**
gear cable: the wire cables that connect the thumb shifts to the derailleur and front gear mechanism

gear ratios: gear ratios are determined by the number of teeth on each cog and chainwheel

grid reference: a position on a map, found by reading off the numbers on the horizontal and vertical grid lines

headset: the place where the handlebar stem fits into the frame. There should be no loose movement

head tube: the short tube that connects the top tube and down tube

head tube angle: the angle between the head tube and the horizontal

high gears: gears for going downhill, using the biggest chainwheel and smallest cog for the highest gear

hub: the free-moving center of the wheel, which revolves on bearings

indexed gears: gear shifters that click from gear to gear

inflate: put air into a tire

inner tube: the light rubber tube that is inflated inside the tire

low gears: gears for going uphill or riding over a tricky trail. The lowest gear uses the smallest chainwheel and the biggest cog

lubricate, lubrication: adding oil to metal mechanical moving parts to allow them to move easily

lugs: a steel sleeve covering where the tubes of a bike frame are joined

panniers: bags carried on each side

quick-release lever: used to attach the wheels to the dropouts and the seat post to the frame for easy adjustment

rear dropouts: see **dropouts**

rear sprocket: the small cogs on the back wheel

reflector: something that reflects car headlights

rolling resistance: the friction caused by the tires. Fat tires have much more rolling resistance than thin tires, but they grip much better

sealed bearings: most off-road bikes have bearings that are enclosed to keep the grease in. They are not totally watertight, so some maintenance is necessary

seat stay: the two narrow tubes connecting the chainstays to the seat tube

seat tube: the tube connecting the bottom bracket to the saddle end of the top tube

seat tube angle: the angle between the seat tube and horizontal

sidewall: side of the tire

slalom: off-road competition usually featuring two riders

spindle: the rod that holds the cranks through the bottom bracket

spoke wrench: specialist tool for tightening spokes

sprockets: rear cogs

stem: the L-shape tube that connects the handlebars to the headset. The length and angle of the stem also govern handling

thumb shift: gear levers that can be shifted by the thumbs

TIG welding: tungsten inert gas welding is used to assemble frames using lugless joins

tire lever: small metal lever used to take tires off wheels

tire pressure: the amount of air that is in the tire

toe straps: straps and clips that hold the feet to the pedals

top tube: the tube connecting the head tube to the seat tube

U-brake: a brake that works on the same principle as the cantilever brake, but is shaped like a U

wheelbase: the horizontal distance between the two wheel hubs

wheelie: kicking the front wheel up in the air, useful for getting over logs

Index

The numbers in **bold** are illustrations

associations 45
all-terrain bike 4

bottom bracket 10, 12, 13, 39, 46
brakes 19, 37, 38, 39, 46
braking 22, **22**, 25

cadence 24, 46
cantilever brakes 5, 10, 46
carrying 8, **8**
chain 13, 35, 38
chainrings 46
chainset 5, 46
chainstays 12, 46
chain tool 33, 35, 39, 46
chainwheel 4, 5, 13, 39, 46
checklist 32
cleaning 36, 37, 38
clothing 14, **14**, 15, **15**, 17, 33
clubs 29
cogs 4, 5, 13, **13**, 46
compass 30, 33
components 7, 46
control 26, **26**, 27, **27**
cornering 22, **22**
crank extractor 39, 46
cranks 5, 13, 38, 46
cro-moly 12, 46
custom bikes 5, 46

dehydration 33, 46
derailleur 38, 46
derailleur jockey wheels 39, 46
derailleur spring 35, 46
down tube 12, 46
drink 33
dropouts 46

eye protection 14, 21

food 33
forks 12, 46

frame shapes 12
freewheel 5, 13, 39, 46
front dropouts 12, 46

gear cables 37, 39, 46
gear ratios 5, 13, 46
gears 4, 5, 6, 13, 19, 24, 38
glasses 21
Gould, Tim 45

handlebars 13, 19, **19**, 22, 23, 25, 26
headset 12, 13, 47
head tube 47
helmet 11, 14, 15, **15**, 17, 18, 40
high gears 24, 47
hillclimbs 43
hubs 10, 47

indexed gears 10, 47
inner tube 33, 34, 47
insurance 19, 40

jumping 27

Kloser, Mike 45
Kluge, Mike 45

lights 17, **17**, 18
locks 19
low gears 23, 24, 47
lubrication 10, 37, 39, **39**, 47
lugs 12, 47

manufacture 7
map reading 30, 31, 33
Mountain Bike Club 29
mud 35, **35**, 36
Mycycles Classic 9, 41

National Off-Road Bicycle Association (NORBA) 11, 29, 44, 45

off-road code 20
Overend, Ned 44, 45

panniers 32, **32**, 47
pedals 13, 39
punctures 33, 34, **34**, 39

quick-release levers 5, 47

racing 40, 41, 42, 43, 44, 45
rear dropouts 12, 47
rear sprockets 37, 47
reflectors 17, 47
Repack 6
rights of way 18, 20
road riding 16, 18
rolling resistance 5, 16, 47

safety 8, 11, 15, 25, 26, 28, 30, 35, 37, 40
sealed bearings 10, 13, 36, 47
seat stays 12, 47
seat tube 12, 47
sidewall 38, 47
size 10, 11
skid turns 22
slalom 43, 47
slipping 24
slow turns 23
snow 7, **7**
spindle 13, 47
spoke wrench 38, 39, 47
sprockets 37, 47
stem 13, 47

theft 19
thumb shifts 5, 16, 47
TIG welding 12, 47
tires 16, 32, 33, 34, 38, 47
toe straps 5, 47
Tomac, John 45
tools 20, 33, 39
top tube 10, 11, 12, 47
trails 9
trials riding 42

U-brake 10, 47
urban bikes 10

wheelbase 12, 47
wheelies 23, **23**, 47

48